W9-ARC-202

INDEPENDENCE DAY

A TRUE BOOK®

by

Nancy I. Sanders

Children's Press®

A Division of Scholastic Inc.

New York Toronto London Auckland Sydney
Mexico City New Delhi Hong Kong
Danbury, Connecticut

SOUTH HUNTINGTON
PUBLIC LIBRARY
HUNTINGTON STATION, NY 11746

R394.26
Sanders

Reading Consultant
Jeanne Clidas, Ph.D.
*National Reading Consultant
and Professor of Reading,
SUNY Brockport*

Content Consultant
Len Travers
*Assistant Professor,
University of Massachusetts,
Dartmouth*

Dedication
For Nathan Layton and his
commitment to serve our
country in the armed forces.

A family watching a
Fourth of July parade

Library of Congress Cataloging-in-Publication Data

Sanders, Nancy I.
  Independence Day / by Nancy I. Sanders.
     p. cm. — (A true book)
Includes bibliographical references (p.) and index.
Contents: Fireworks spectacular—The history of a nation—The
Revolutionary War—Across the years—Life, liberty, and the pursuit
of happiness.
  ISBN 0-516-22764-5 (lib. bdg.)   0-516-27778-2 (pbk.)
  1. Fourth of July—Juvenile literature. 2. Fourth of July
celebrations—Juvenile literature. [1. Fourth of July. 2. Holidays.]
I. Title. II. Series.
  E286.A163 2003
  394.2634—dc21

                                2003004526

© 2003 by Scholastic Inc.
All rights reserved. Published simultaneously in Canada.
Printed in the United States of America.

CHILDREN'S PRESS, and A TRUE BOOK®, and associated logos are
trademarks and or registered trademarks of Scholastic Library Publishing.
SCHOLASTIC and associated logos are trademarks and or registered
trademarks of Scholastic Inc.

1 2 3 4 5 6 7 8 9 10 R 12 11 10 09 08 07 06 05 04 03

3065200136 7897

Contents

Fireworks over the U.S. Capitol in Washington, D.C.

Fireworks Spectacular

Sparkle! Fizzle! Pop, bang, boom! Fireworks light up the night sky on the Fourth of July. Everyone claps and cheers. What a wonderful sight!

Every summer, Americans join together to celebrate the birthday of their country. Families and friends get

Many families celebrate the Fourth of July by having picnics or barbecues (right) or attending Fourth of July parades (below).

together for picnics or barbecues. People roast hot dogs,
drink lemonade, and eat
apple pie. Kids play baseball.
At Fourth of July parades,
bands march down the streets
playing **patriotic** songs.

Then the sun begins to set.
It gets dark. Everyone waits
excitedly for the show to
begin. Finally, fireworks begin
to explode in the sky. Happy
birthday to the United States
of America!

The Beginnings of a Nation

After Christopher Columbus sailed to the Americas in the late 1400s, other countries in Europe sent explorers to North and South America. In 1607, settlers from England built the first permanent English **colony** in what is now the United States.

Jamestown in the early 1600s

Jamestown was located in the area known today as Virginia. The colonists worked hard to stay alive in the wild, new land.

Companies in England sent more people to North America to build more towns. The companies wanted the colonists to produce raw materials for English factories to use. It was a hard life and many workers were needed.

For the chance of a new life, many poor people came to the colonies as indentured servants. In exchange for free passage to the colonies, these people had to work for a number of years without pay before being given their freedom.

Still more workers were needed. Many Africans were kidnapped from their home-lands, brought to the colonies, and forced into slavery. A few American Indians were forced to become slaves as well.

Over time, people from England and other European countries settled thirteen colonies along the eastern

The thirteen colonies (left) were ruled by King George III of England (below).

coast. Each colony had its own government, but these governments were controlled by the king of England.

England made laws that the American colonists felt were unfair. The colonists were not allowed to vote on decisions made by the English government that affected the daily lives of the colonists. They were forced to pay extra **taxes** on goods such as tea, spices, and fabric. When the

In 1773, in what became known as the Boston Tea Party, American colonists dumped tea into Boston Harbor to protest a British tax on tea.

American colonists complained, the English government ignored them. The colonists began to ignore the laws, and refused to pay the taxes.

Finally, King George III sent armed soldiers from England to the colonies to force the colonists to obey the laws. Alarmed, a group of colonial leaders known as the First Continental Congress met in Philadelphia in 1774. The members talked with each other about the problems with England. They discussed what should be done to protect their freedom and rights.

The colonists prepared to fight. They secretly gathered guns and weapons. Men volunteered to be minutemen— colonists who were ready to fight at a minute's notice. Slaves and free African-Americans volunteered to fight as well.

In 1775, British troops marched toward Concord, Massachusetts. The troops wanted to capture a supply of weapons hidden there. Minutemen tried to stop them at the North Bridge in Concord.

Minutemen trying to stop the British from crossing the North Bridge at Concord

"The shot heard 'round the world" was fired by the minutemen, and the Revolutionary War against England began.

The Revolutionary War

The Continental Congress met again. It called together colonists to form the Continental Army. George Washington was chosen to lead this army.

During the war, American leader Thomas Jefferson

A painting showing Thomas Jefferson (standing), Benjamin Franklin (left), and John Adams (center) working on the Declaration of Independence

prepared a special document. It stated that the colonies wanted independence—to no longer be ruled by England.

Jefferson included important ideas about freedom in this Declaration of Independence. On July 4, 1776, members of the Continental Congress approved the Declaration of

The Declaration of Independence was approved by the Continental Congress on July 4, 1776.

People gathering to hear the Declaration of Independence read aloud in Boston

Independence. A few days later, Americans bravely rang the Liberty Bell in Philadelphia. Crowds gathered to hear the

Declaration of Independence read aloud.

The Revolutionary War was long and hard. British troops were well-trained soldiers with powerful guns. The colonists' troops were made up mainly of untrained men with few supplies and weapons. But General Washington led his army well, even through long, hard winters. After nearly eight years, the war was over. The colonists had won and a

General Washington held his troops together through several harsh winters (below), and eventually the Americans won the war against the British.

new country was born: the United States of America.

The Declaration of Independence

We hold these truths to be self-evident, that all men are created equal, that they are **endowed** by their Creator with certain **unalienable** Rights, that among these are Life, Liberty and the pursuit of Happiness.

—famous words from the Declaration of Independence

Who wrote it?
Written largely by Thomas Jefferson, with some help from other members of the Continental Congress

Thomas Jefferson

Who signed it?
Representatives from each of the thirteen colonies at the Continental Congress, including John Hancock, Benjamin Franklin, and John Adams

Where is it today?
The National Archives in Washington, D.C.

Through the Years

Independence Day has been celebrated every year since the Declaration of Independence was approved. On July 4, 1777, just one year later, Americans gathered in Philadelphia. Bells were rung, bands played, and ships fired their cannons. At night,

bonfires were lit and fireworks exploded in the sky.

Over the years, other historic events have taken place on the

The cornerstone for the Washington Monument was set in place on July 4, 1848. This photo shows the monument today.

Fourth of July. On July 4, 1848, the **cornerstone** for the Washington Monument was set in place in Washington, D.C. This monument was built to remember and honor George Washington, the first president of the United States.

On July 4, 1876, The United States of America celebrated its one-hundredth birthday, or centennial. A world's fair called the Centennial Exposition was held in Philadelphia to honor

In July 4, 1876, the United States celebrated its one-hundredth birthday (right). That year, the torch of the not-yet-finished Statue of Liberty was displayed at the Centennial Exposition in Philadelphia (below).

this important event. The purpose of the fair was to show the progress the United States had made since its founding. People flocked to the fair to see art exhibits and displays of new farming products, manufactured products, and inventions.

On July 4, 1881, Booker T. Washington opened the school that would become Tuskegee Institute, a college dedicated to educating African-Americans. By that

On July 4, 1881, Booker T. Washington (right) opened the school that would become Tuskegee Institute.

time, the Civil War was over and slavery had been outlawed. In its early days, Tuskegee Institute taught a variety of subjects, with a focus on practical education. Students learned skills such as shoemaking, farming, construction, and printing.

A poem that was to become a much-loved American song was published on July 4, 1895. Katharine Lee Bates had traveled

On July 4, 1895, Katharine Lee Bates (left) published a poem that would someday become a famous American song (below).

America the Beautiful

O beautiful for spacious skies,
For amber waves of grain,
For purple mountains majestic
Above the fruited plain!
America! America!
God shed His grace on thee
And crown thy good with brotherhood
From sea to shining sea!

O beautiful for pilgrim feet
Whose stern, impassioned stress
A thoroughfare for freedom beat
Across the wilderness!
America! America!
God mend thine every flaw,
Confirm thy soul in self-control,
Thy liberty in law!

O beautiful for heroes proved
In liberating strife,
Who more than self their country loved
And mercy more than life!
America! America!
May God thy gold refine
Till all success be nobleness
And every gain divine!

O beautiful for patriot dream
That sees beyond the years
Thine alabaster cities gleam
Undimmed by human tears!
America! America!
God shed His grace on thee
And crown thy good with brotherhood
From sea to shining sea!

Katharine Lee Bates

across parts of the United States and was **inspired** to write about its beauty. Her poem, "America the Beautiful," was put to music in 1910. Today, schoolchildren all over the country sing this song.

On July 4, 1976, the United States celebrated its two-hundredth birthday, or bicentennial. One of the most famous events was Operation Sail in New York City. Majestic, tall ships from around the world sailed through New York

Operation Sail, in New York Harbor, was part of the U.S. bicentennial celebration in 1976.

Harbor. Millions of people watched from the shore. After the spectacular parade finished, fireworks lit up the night sky.

Symbols of Freedom

The American flag has thirteen red and white stripes that represent the original colonies. It has fifty stars, one for each state.

The Liberty Bell is a symbol of freedom.

The bald eagle is the national bird of the United States.

The Statue of Liberty stands in New York Harbor to welcome people to the United States.

"The Star-Spangled Banner," written by Francis Scott Key, is the national anthem of the United States.

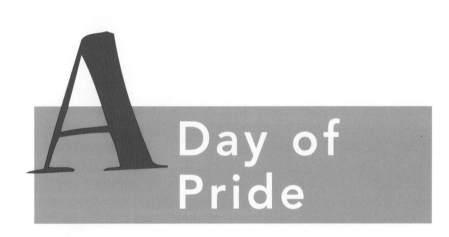

A Day of Pride

Ever since the United States was founded, people have moved there in search of freedom. People have come to the country to live under a government that is elected by the people. This gives all **citizens** the opportunity to have a say in how they are governed. People

European immigrants arriving in the United States in the early 1900s

have come in search of religious freedom. They have left friends and family behind to move to the United States to begin new lives. Independence Day celebrates the freedom people have in the United States.

Independence Day is a holiday when families and communities show their pride in their country. Many towns and cities have patriotic parades. Firefighters, police officers, and other community helpers march on foot or drive their vehicles down the street.

Veterans—soldiers who fought in wars to protect the United States—march in the parades as well. People dress in colonial-style clothes or wear outfits of red, white,

Firefighters waving from an antique fire truck during a Fourth of July parade (above) and Americans showing their pride in their country on Independence Day (left)

and blue. They wave American flags at the parades and fly flags outside their homes.

After dark, huge fireworks displays explode in the sky. Everyone claps and cheers. Independence Day is a day to be thankful for the freedom available to people living in the United States of America. It is also a day to hope for freedom for all people around the world.

To Find Out More

Here are some additional resources to help you learn more about Independence Day:

 **Books**

Curlee, Lynn. **Liberty.** Atheneum, 2000.

Gore, Willma. **Independence Day.** Enslow Publishers, 1993.

Landau, Elaine. **Independence Day: Birthday of the United States.** Enslow Publishers, 2001.

Quiri, Patricia Ryon. **The American Flag** (True Books). Children's Press, 1998.

Ross, Alice. **The Copper Lady.** Carolrhoda Books, 1997.

Swanson, June. **I Pledge Allegiance.** Carolrhoda Books, 1991.

Fourth of July— Independence Day

http://www.usacitylink. com/usa/

Learn about American history and find out about the United States today. Follow links to visit the White House, other governmental offices, and your state's home page.

The Greatest American Fourth of July— Operation Sail

http://www.pbs.org/wnet/ julyfourth/sail.html

See the majestic tall ships that sailed in New York Harbor on Independence Day in 1976.

Happy Fourth of July!

http://www.geocities.com/ EnchantedForest/Dell/ 7002/July4.html

Listen to patriotic music as you have fun on this colorful, informative, and fun site. You can also watch a fireworks show and learn important tips to make your holiday safe.

Kids Domain— July Fourth Fun

http://www.kidsdomain. com/holiday/july4

Watch electronic fireworks, print out puzzles and activities, play online holiday games, and get patriotic clip art.

National Archives and Records Administration

http://www.nara.gov

At this website, you can visit the online Exhibit Hall to read the Declaration of Independence. You can also learn about the Founding Fathers who signed this important document.

Important Words

citizens people who belong to a country and are protected by its laws

colony group of people living in a new land who are ruled by the government of another country

cornerstone stone laid at the corner of a building to mark the start of construction

endowed supplied

inspired filled with desire to do something

patriotic having or showing love, loyalty, or devotion to one's country

representatives people chosen to voice the opinions of other people

taxes money people pay to support the government

unalienable cannot be taken away

Index

Meet the Author

Independence Day has always been a favorite holiday for Nancy I. Sanders. She was sixteen years old when the United States celebrated its bicentennial. Nancy's mother and older sister sewed Nancy a pilgrim's dress. She wore it in a patriotic parade, marching with friends down the main street of her hometown, Everett, Pennsylvania.

Today, Nancy enjoys writing about exciting moments in the history of the United States. She has written more than fifty books, including several other True Books and *A Kid's Guide to African American History* (Chicago Review Press). Nancy and her husband, Jeff, live in California with their two sons, Dan and Ben.

Photographs © 2003: Bridgeman Art Library International Ltd., London/New York: 12 right, 19; Corbis Images: 37 top (Theo Allofs), 14, 17, 21, 23, 39 (Bettman), 43 (Firefly Productions), 1 (John Henley), 36 bottom (Bob Krist), 35 (Charles E. Rotkin), 4 (Pete Saloutos), 28 (Alan Schein Photography), cover, 6 top (Ariel Skelley), 24 (Joseph Sohm; Visions of America), 37 bottom (UPI), 30 left, 32; Falmouth Historical Society: 33 right, 33 left; Hulton|Archive/Getty Images: 9, 25 top; North Wind Picture Archives: 20, 27, 30 right; PhotoEdit: 41 top (Gary Conner), 2 (Tony Freeman), 41 bottom (Jeff Greenberg), 6 bottom, 25 bottom (John Neubauer), 37 center (Jonathan Nourok); The Image Works: 36 top (Rob Crandall), 12 left.